To

....

....

....

....

....

From

....

FREE BONUS

Get your FREE
mini-ebook download

*The Handy Little Book of
Awesome Bad Dad Jokes*

✔ Includes over 50 dad jokes and puns

✔ More eye-rolls and entertainment
   for the whole family.

**Claim your FREE ebook at
www.riddlesandgiggles.com/dad**

Or scan with your phone to
get your free download

Like our Facebook page
@RiddlesandGiggles

Follow us on Instagram
@RiddlesandGiggles_Official

Questions & Customer Service
hello@riddlesandgiggles.com

Dad Jokes Book

by Riddles and Giggles™

www.riddlesandgiggles.com

TABLE OF CONTENTS

INTRODUCTION

"Oh my gosh, Dad. That was such a lame joke."

Fathers, have we heard this phrase before? How about something such as, "Lay off the dad jokes...Dad!" or "If I hear one more dad joke, I'm going to rip out your chest hair!" Starting to sound familiar?

The dad joke is somehow the most universally loved and hated type of humor found in human culture. Although they're called dad jokes, anyone can tell them. Moms and kids tell them to family and friends, but we call them dad jokes because they're more commonly delivered by a dad.

When executed correctly, dad jokes can become the hit of the family party or make you the "cool dad" at your kid's sleepover. Even the worst dad jokes always have a chance of tipping the scales so far that they enter the "so bad it was good" territory. So, if you are able to reach either of the extremes (great dad joke or so-bad-it-was-good dad joke), you will immediately become the hit of the gathering.

The most important thing to understand about dad jokes is that they are the birthright of all dads. Fathers of all kinds – both biological and non-biological – are immediately given the powerful staff of dad joke power. Remember, wield this staff with care.

The idea of a dad joke is to be non-offensive yet wise, immature yet grand, and hilarious yet subdued. Like the aura of dads in general, the dad joke is not meant to "steal the thunder" from the other people in the room. No, it is to add a steady trickle of water to an already constant stream of good entertainment. A good dad joke adds but never subtracts; multiplies but never divides. In other words, it pleases the math-es, I mean masses. Use your power for good, but never let it go to your head.

Now, what exactly does a good dad joke entail? Well, it varies. The most common dad jokes that you come across are puns, one-liners, or just a joke – told by dads – that can entertain kids or adults of any age.

Inside is a collection of funny, corny, and laugh-out-loud (or quietly to yourself) dad jokes that you can inflict on unsuspecting kids, family, and adults alike. Like any good book, this collection of jokes can be used in any situation to create a laugh. Awkward business gathering? Dad jokes. The magician doesn't show up to your kid's birthday party? Dad jokes. Mom's book club night? Dad jokes. This book is the wand to your Harry Potter, the Toto to your Dorothy, and the lukewarm beer to your Sunday night BBQ—it fits every situation imaginable.

So, strap in and prepare to cause some tears (of joy... hopefully), eye-rolls, illicit groans, or a slight smile. Job done.

CLASSIC Q&A JOKES

CLASSIC Q&A JOKES

This is probably the one time in the history of humanity where something with the phrase "Q&A" in it will be fun. Don't think of a celebrity YouTube video or business meeting here. No, the Q&A joke – a joke type held in high esteem within the tool-belt of any strong dad joker – will quickly become your best friend. The goal of this type of joke, quite simply, is to answer a question. Think of it as a call and response, if you will. The first line of the joke details a question: Why did the chicken cross the road? And the second half of the joke responds: because all of the KFCs were making him uncomfortable. Easy. Enjoy these classic morsels of hilarity. You're welcome.

. . . .

What did the right eye say to the left eye? **"Between you and me, something smells."**

Why did the shopping cart quit? **It was tired of being pushed around.**

What's the worst thing about being a Uber driver? **All those people talking behind your back.**

Why is 16 always full? **Because it 8 and 8.**

What has four wheels and flies? **A garbage truck.**

How do two salesmen say farewell to each other? **"Buy!"**

Why was the teenager staring at the orange juice container? **It said concentrate.**

Daughter
Dad, have you been to Prague?

Dad
No, but I've always wanted to Czech it out.

Why was the Kit Kat sad? **Because his Dad was wafer so long.**

What do you call a ship that just wants to fit in? **A membership.**

Why did the birthday boy wrap himself in paper? **He wanted to live in the present.**

What do you call an elephant that doesn't matter? **An irrelephant.**

What happened to the movie trailer? **I don't know—it was last scene just moments ago...**

> **Boss**
> How good are you at Powerpoint?

> **Dad**
> I Excel at it.

> **Boss**
> Was that a pun?

> **Dad**
> Word.

What did one plate whisper to the other plate? **"Dinner is on me."**

Why can't you hear psychics go to the bathroom? **Because the "p" is silent.**

How much do you pay for dead batteries? **Nothing, they're free of charge.**

When is a car not a car? **When it turns into a driveway.**

How can you tell that a pickle is getting old? **When his days are cucumbered.**

What do you call grass with a potty mouth? **Crass.**

How many teaching applicants did we have this year at our Catholic school? **Nun.**

Why is it bad to iron your four-leaf clover? **Because you shouldn't press your luck.**

Want to hear a joke about construction? **I'm still working on it.**

Why couldn't the toilet paper cross the road? **It got stuck in a crack.**

Daughter
Dad, is it safe to dive into the pool?

Dad
It deep ends.

What is the hardest part of learning how to ride a bicycle? **The pavement.**

What did the drummer call his twin daughters? **Anna One, Anna Two.**

What do you call a kangaroo in a lot of trouble? **Sc-roo-d.**

Why was the poker player kicked out of the casino? **He was turning the tables.**

What did the penny want to be when it grew up? **A copper.**

What did the salad say when the refrigerator door was opened? **"Close the door. I'm dressing!"**

Why did the fisherman order the halibut? **Just for the halibut.**

What did the shy pebble wish for?
That he could be a little boulder.

Son: Dad, are we pyromaniacs?
Dad: Yes, we arson.

What do you call cheese that
isn't yours? **Nacho cheese.**

What did the trash yell when
it was scared? **Holy scrap.**

Why can't a leopard hide?
Because he's always spotted.

What did Jay-Z call his wife before
he married her? **Feyonce.**

What's ET short for? **Because he's got little legs.**

What's the most relaxed Mexican food? **En-chill-adas.**

How do lemons answer the phone? *"Yellow!"*

What did the sink tell the toilet? **You look flushed.**

How do you signal the start of a reading race? **On your bookmarks, get set, go!**

Why did the computer get mad at the printer? **It didn't like its toner voice.**

What do you call a bad guy who finds his way? **A convert.**

Daughter: Dad, did you ever win "employee of the month?"
Dad: Yes, once I became the employer.

What's another name for a veggie platter? **Gross-eries.**

What do you call a man who can't stand up? **Neil.**

Why didn't the stick of dynamite go off? **It found itself confused.**

Why shouldn't you give Elsa a kite? **Because she'll let it go.**

What do you call a group of musicians who are no longer allowed to play together? **Banned.**

Why did the video game monster run away from home? **Her parents kept trying to controller.**

What did the mountain climber name his son? **Cliff.**

Why are hairdressers always on time?
They know all the short cuts.

What do you call a magician
who loses his magic? **Ian.**

What do you call a man with
a rubber toe? **Roberto.**

What's gravity's favorite season? **Fall.**

> **Son**
> Dad, what makes a really good tongue twister?

> **Dad**
> Well, it's hard to say.

Why did the donut go to the dentist? **To get a filling.**

What do you call a pair of kidneys that like things neat? **Organ-ized.**

What kind of car does a sheep like to drive? **A lamborghini.**

What do you call an alligator wearing a vest? **An investigator.**

Why did the orange lose the race? **It ran out of juice.**

What's the opposite of artificial intelligence? **Natural stupidity.**

What's the difference between a hippo and a Zippo? **One is very heavy; the other is a little lighter.**

What do you call a guy with a car on his head? **Jack.**

Daughter
Dad, I want an astronomy theme for my birthday.

Dad
Ok, let's planet.

Why did the man get fired from the bank on his first day? **He pushed a customer who asked to check their balance.**

What's the difference between ignorance and apathy? **I don't know and I don't care.**

What's Forrest Gump's email password? **1forest1.**

Why did the spoon come to the party dressed as a knife? **The invitation said to look sharp.**

What is water's favorite
type of dance? **Tap.**

Why did the chicken go to the
séance? **To get to the other side.**

What do you call a man with no
arms or legs at the door? **Matt.**

What happens if you swallow a dictionary? **You'll get thesaurus throat you've ever had.**

Son
Dad, what's the difference between a numerator and a denominator?

Dad
A short line, but only a fraction of people know that.

Why are bowling pins depressed?
They're always getting knocked down.

What did the fried rice say to the egg? **Don't wok away from me.**

Why are Russian babushka dolls so stuck up? **They are full of themselves.**

What do you call a polite person who builds bridges? **A civil engineer.**

What did the nut yell when it was chasing another nut? **"I'm a cashew."**

What do you call a can opener that's broken? **A can't opener.**

What did the paper say to the pen? **"Write on, man!"**

Why were the utensils stuck together? **They were spooning.**

Son
Dad, where do you buy broth from?

Dad
The stock market.

What did the sock say to make the foot go away? **Shoe!**

What does the ocean use to
do its laundry? **Tide.**

How do lawyers say
goodbye? **"Sue ya soon!"**

What's the fundamental difference
between a bad joke and a
dad joke? **The first letter.**

"DID YOU HEAR...?"

"DID YOU HEAR..." JOKES

Similar in theory to the classic Q&A jokes, "Did you hear..." jokes are two-line jokes that begin with "Did you hear...?"

This makes it quite easy to rattle off quickly a number of these types of jokes, as the punchlines can sometimes be similar. Don't underestimate these guys, though—although they may seem simpler to set up and execute than their Q&A counterparts, these jokes can still pack quite the comic punch.

. . . .

Did you hear about the population growth in Ireland? **It's Dublin.**

Did you hear about the business making boats in the attic? **Sails have been going through the roof.**

Did you hear about the power outlet that trashed-talked to the power cord? **It thought it could socket to him.**

Did you hear about the rare, secret ability of that video game character? **It gives you the power to get up and go outside.**

Did you hear about the shoe factory fire? **Thousands of soles were lost.**

Did you hear the joke about wrapping paper? **Never mind—it's tear-able.**

Did you hear the joke about the electrician? **I can't tell you—it's too shocking.**

Did you hear that they are going to ban youth sports? **Yes, apparently they are distracting children from their TikTok careers.**

Did you hear how the mountain got over its depression? **It changed its altitude.**

Did you hear about the circus fire? **It was in tents.**

Did you hear about the mannequin that lost all of his friends? **Yeah, he was too clothes-minded.**

Did you hear about the guy who wanted a replacement wife? **Not only did he fail to get it, but he lost the original.**

Did you hear about that noise complaint? **What did you say?**

Did you hear the funny joke about the boomerang? **I forgot, but I'm sure it'll come back to me.**

Did you hear about the claustrophobic astronaut? **He just wanted a bit more space.**

Did you hear about the child that wanted to become a monster? **The mom said they were already doing a great job.**

Did you hear about the square that got into a car accident? **Yeah, now he's a rect-angle.**

Did you hear about the assault rifle that started the race too early? **It jumped the gun.**

Did you hear the joke about German sausages? **Oh man, it's the wurst.**

Did you hear about the man who was buried alive? **It was a grave mistake.**

Did you hear about the gate that spent too much time in the sun? **Yeah, it was quite the golden gate.**

Did you hear about the ATM that got addicted to money? **It suffered from withdrawals.**

Did you hear about the cross-eyed teacher? **He couldn't control his pupils.**

Did you hear about Mal? **Yes, but I could never figure out Mal's function...his equipment always seemed to be breaking.**

Did you hear about the angry
paleontologist? **She had a bone to pick.**

Did you hear about the banana
that snored loudly? **It woke
up the whole bunch.**

Did you hear about the married couple
that hated each other? **They've been
happily married for thirty-five years.**

Did you hear about the guy whose whole left arm got amputated? **He's all right now.**

Did you hear about the sausage shop that closed down? **Yeah, it couldn't make ends meat.**

Did you hear about the politician who wasn't just looking for power? **No.**

Did you hear about burglars being quite sensitive? **It's because they take things personally.**

Did you hear about the guy who invented Altoids? **They say he made a mint.**

Did you hear about the number that couldn't keep still? **It was a roam-ing numeral.**

Did you hear about the twig that couldn't cook a marshmallow? **It kept getting the short end of the stick.**

Did you hear the joke about the roof? **Never mind, it's over your head.**

Did you hear about the guy who invented the knock-knock joke? **He won the "no-bell" prize.**

Did you hear about the semicolon that got arrested? **He got two consecutive sentences.**

Did you hear about the child who exhibited good patience? **Yes, I read fairy tales.**

Did you hear about the lumberjack who got a promotion? **Now he's a branch manager.**

Did you hear about the world tongue-twister champion getting arrested? **I hear they're going to give him a really tough sentence.**

Did you hear about the cheese factory explosion? **There was nothing left but de-brie.**

Did you hear that the person who invented Halls cough drops has died? **Apparently, there will be no coffin at his funeral.**

KNOCK-KNOCK JOKES

KNOCK-KNOCK JOKES

Ah, the knock-knock joke. Used particularly often back in our middle school days to incite a cheap laugh from a friend or a stern look from a teacher, the knock-knock joke never hesitates to amaze with its simplistic beauty. Anyone can create them, yes, but to pen a truly special knock-knock joke is to discover a true piece of art. The knock-knock joke is the joke-of-all...sorry, jack-of-all-trades for the dad joke community. Enjoy these sassy, wisecracking knock-knock jokes and keep these suckers nearby for visitors at your next gathering.

. . . .

Knock, knock.
Who's there?
Yeah.
Yeah who?
Whoa, take it easy there, Cowboy.

Knock, knock.
Who's there?
Water.
Water who?
Water doing? Just open the door!

Knock, knock.
Who's there?
You.
You who?
Seriously, Terry? We've been friends for years.

Knock, knock.
Who's there?
Burglar.
Burglar who?
Burglars don't knock.

Knock, knock.
Who's there?
Iva.
Iva who?
I've a sore hand from knocking, so open up!

Knock, knock.
Who's there?
A Brazilian model.
Well, by all means, come in!

Knock, knock.
Who's there?
Guess.
Guess who?
No, that's your job.

Knock, knock.
Who's there?
Ice cream soda.
Ice cream soda who?
Ice scream soda neighbors
can hear mEEEeee.

Knock, knock.
Who's there?
Danger.
Danger who?
You opened the door? I even
told you there was danger!

Knock, knock.
Who's there?
Cabbage.
Cabbage who?
You expect a cabbage to have a last name?

Knock, knock.
Who's there?
Daisy.
Daisy who?
Daisy me rollin, they hatin'...

Knock, knock.
Who's there?
Nanotechnology.
Nanotechnology who?
I don't know. I'm still trying to wrap
my head around that word.

Knock, knock.
Who's there?
FBI.
FB...
Excuse me, sir, we're asking
the questions here.

Knock, knock.
Who's there?
Amazon.
Amazon who?
Listen, kid, I don't get paid enough for
this. Do you want the package or not?

Knock, knock.
Who's there?
Yah.
Yah who?
Nah, thanks. I much prefer Google

Knock, knock.
Who's there?
Scotch.
Scotch who?
Ehh, I'm more of a whisky guy.

Knock, knock.
Who's there?
Opportunity.
Don't be silly...are you for real?
Opportunity doesn't knock twice.

Knock, knock.
Who's there?
Platonic.
Platonic who?
I know, where's the fun in that?

Knock, knock.
Who's there?
Ida.
Ida who?
Dude, it's pronounced Idaho.

Knock, knock.
Who's there?
T-Rex.
T-Rex who?
Seriously, there's a T-Rex at your door
and you want to know his name!?!

Knock, knock.
Who's there?
A pile-up.
A pile-up who?
Ewwwwww.

Knock, knock.
Who's there?
Heave.
Heave who?
Dude, some pirate you are...it's "heave ho!"

Knock, knock.
Who's there?
An ugly guy.
...
That's what I thought.

Knock, knock.
Who's there?
Some.
Some who?
Some wise guy who thinks he's
funny being a knock-knock joke.

Knock, knock.
Who's there?
June.
June who?
June know how long I've been
knocking out here?

Knock, knock.
Who's there?
Who.
Who who?
Whooooooo are you...who who, who who...

Knock, knock.
Who's there?
Chipped.
Chipped who?
Not chipped who, a chipped tooth! It
has to be around here somewhere...

Knock, knock.
Who's there?
Sorry.
Sorry who?
Sorry, wrong door.

Knock, knock.
Who's there?
Fill.
Fill who?
I don't know, Jamie. Who's Phil?!
Is there another man?

Knock, knock.
Who's there?
No one.
No one who?
Remains silent

ONE-LINERS AND PUNS

ONE-LINERS & PUNS

If knock-knock jokes are the "jack-of-all-trades" of the dad joke community, then one-liners and puns are the MVP. Short, sweet, and infinitely humorous, one-liners and puns are wordplay at its finest.

More importantly than that, though, is the fact that these can be deployed in quite truly every situation imaginable. They have no setup, are not long-winded, and are nearly guaranteed to garner at least a chuckle.

As it usually goes in literature, we have saved the best for last. *Mic drop*.

. . . .

I accidentally handed my wife the superglue instead of her lipstick. She still isn't talking to me.

I used to be addicted to the hokey pokey, but then I turned myself around.

My girlfriend works at the zoo. I think she's a keeper.

It's probably not safe for me to be driving right now. But, hey, bad brakes have never stopped me before.

My friend asked me, "What's the best part about living in Switzerland?" I said, "I don't know, but the flag is a big plus."

Ladies, if your boyfriend doesn't appreciate your fruit jokes, you need to let that mango.

I sympathize with batteries. I'm never included in anything either.

I heard a man in the woods yelling "Help, bear!" That's so odd. If I needed help, a bear would be the last thing I'd call for.

I wanted to go on a diet, but I feel like I have way too much on my plate right now.

They say that 3/2 people
are bad at fractions.

Dad
I think I have a "dad bod."

Daughter
To me, it's more like a father figure.

Welcome to our restaurant. Do
you have a reservation? No, it's
OK. I'm sure I want to eat here.

A police officer caught two kids stealing a car battery and a firework. He charged one and let the other one off.

My mates and I started a band called "999 Megabytes." We still haven't gotten a gig.

I don't want to brag, but I finished the puzzle in a week, and it said "2 to 4 years" on the box.

My wife thinks I don't give her enough privacy. At least that's what she said in her diary.

To the person who stole my place in the queue—I'm after you now.

I have a joke about drilling, but it's boring.

I have a joke about procrastination, but I'll tell you later.

I have a few jokes about retired people, but none of them work.

I have kleptomania. When it gets really bad, I take something for it.

I had a joke about Nirvana,
but Nevermind.

I have a joke about chemistry, but I
don't think it will get much of a reaction.

I have this great joke about amnesia,
but I forgot how it goes.

A book just fell on my head. I've only got my shelf to blame.

A priest, a pastor, and a rabbit walk into a blood bank. The rabbit says, "I think I might be a type o."

Interviewer: What's your greatest strength? Dad: I can perform under pressure. Interviewer: Great, can you give me an example? Dad: "Sure." *Takes a deep breath, clicks fingers, and sings* "Pressure, under pressure..."

I once had a turtle for a teacher; he tortoise well.

Don't make your password "beef stew." It's not stroganoff.

I tried to phone the ladder company, but it just rung and rung.

DAD JOKES BOOK

Last night, I dreamed I was swimming in an ocean of orange soda, but it was just a Fanta sea.

Finally, my winter fat has gone. Now, I have spring rolls.

I just purchased a book on addiction. I read it 12 times.

Seven days without a pun
makes one weak.

I am terrified of elevators. I'm going
to start taking steps to avoid them.

My printer's name is Jimi Hendrix.
Because it's always jammin'.

I went to a psychic; I knocked on her front door. She yelled, "Who is it?" So I left.

I saw an ad that said, "Radio for sale, $2. Volume stuck on full." I thought to myself, "I can't turn that down."

I bought a wooden car last week. Wooden engine, wooden doors, wooden wheels, wooden seats— the works.
Put the wooden key in the wooden ignition. Wooden start.

I named my horse Mayo. Mayo neighs.

Son
Dad, can you tell me what
a solar eclipse is?

Dad
No sun.

My wife hates it when I mess with
her red wine. I added some fruit
and now she's sangria than ever.

I asked the librarian if the new books about paranoia were available. She looked up and whispered, "They're right behind you."

I tried a career as a lumberjack once. I couldn't hack it, so they gave me the ax.

How do parents lose their kids in a mall? Seriously, any tips are welcome...

No matter how much you push the envelope, it'll still be stationary.

My colleagues are like Christmas lights. Half of them don't work and the other half aren't that bright.

The golf ball wanted to hang out with all its friends, but it couldn't find a fairway to do so.

Not to brag, but I have this incredible talent for predicting what's inside a wrapped present. It's a gift.

The rotation of the Earth really makes my day.

I would like to be a millionaire just like my dad. He always wanted to be a millionaire too.

My wife just accused me of having zero empathy. I just don't understand why she feels that way.

There was a significant cyber attack recently. The government is still looking for the hacker. I think he ran some ware.

Thanks for telling me the meaning of the word "plethora." It really means a lot.

When I visit Italy, I like to Rome around.

I'm working on a new invention that will read minds. I'd love to hear your thoughts.

Someone threw a bottle of omega 3 pills at me. Luckily, my injuries were only super fish oil.

I used to hate facial hair.
Then it grew on me.

In college, I was so broke I couldn't
pay the electricity bill. Those were
the darkest days of my life.

I was having a discussion with a
bank that was going nowhere, so I
told him to just cut to the Chase.

My son does his multiplication homework on the floor because his teacher told him not to use tables.

To the person who stole my glasses—I will use my contacts to find you.

My wife discovered that I replaced our bed with a trampoline. She was so mad she hit the roof.

(Reversing the car) "Ahh, this takes me back."

I can't believe my neighbor knocked on my door at 3:00 a.m.! Luckily, I was already awake practicing the drums.

The wedding was so beautiful— even the cake was in tiers.

Saturday and Sunday are the strongest days. The rest are weekdays.

Someone glued my deck of cards together—I don't know how to deal with it.

I went to the store to pick up eight cans of Sprite. But when I got home, I realized I'd only picked 7Up.

My teachers told me I'd never amount to much since I procrastinate so much. I told them, "Just you wait!"

Mom is mad at me because she asked me to sync her phone, so I threw it in the lake.

I watched a show about how boats are constructed. It was riveting.

My least favorite color is purple. I dislike it more than red and blue combined.

My IQ test results came back. They were negative.

Dear Math, it's time to grow up and solve your own problems.

I was having trouble fastening my seatbelt...and then it just clicked.

Every night, I have a hard time remembering something, but then it dawns on me.

I had to sell my vacuum cleaner. All it was doing was gathering dust.

RIP boiling water—you will be mist.

My wife and I laugh about how competitive we are. But I laugh more.

The milk was caught in class for not reading the whole story—he just skimmed it.

There I was this morning, sitting
and drinking coffee in my slippers;
I thought to myself...I really
need to clean some mugs.

My three favorite things are eating
my family and not using commas.

I sat down at a restaurant and the server
immediately asked if I wanted dessert.
I told him that's the last thing I want.

Bigfoot is sometimes confused for Sasquatch—Yeti never complains.

I received a compliment on my driving today. They even left me a note on my windshield saying, "Parking Fine."

The past, present, and future walk into a bar. It was tense.

Don't interrupt Mom when she's working on a word puzzle. Chances are you'll hear some crosswords.

I accidentally ate cat food. Don't ask meow.

Dogs can't operate MRI machines, but catscan.

My wife said, "Don't get upset if someone calls you fat. You're much bigger than that!"

I'm bad with four things... faces, names, and numbers.

Daughter: Quick, Dad, stop the car. I need to use the bathroom.
Dad: Whoa, sounds like urine trouble there.

I wanted to tell a carpentry joke. I couldn't find any that woodwork.

Do you want to buy a broken air compressor? No pressure.

I spent $500 to hire a limo with no driver. All that money and nothing to chauffeur it.

I was wondering why the Frisbee kept looking larger and larger, and then it hit me.

Learning how to collect trash wasn't hard. I just picked it up as I went along.

I like waiters—they bring a lot to the table.

Shout out to anyone who knows
how to fix broken hinges...
my door's always open.

My boss told me to have a
good day, so I went home.

I have a fear of speed bumps.
I'm slowly getting over it.

I lost my mood ring the other day.
I'm not sure how I feel about it.

I talk to myself because sometimes
I just need expert advice.

My wife refuses to go to karaoke
with me, so I have to duet alone.

I used to think I was indecisive.
But now I'm not so sure.

The cigar wanted to make it big,
but his friends kept telling him
it was just a pipe dream.

I used to play piano by ear.
Now I use my hands.

My girlfriend accidentally poked my eyes...so I stopped seeing her for a while.

I was fired from the keyboard factory today because I wasn't putting in enough shifts.

Air used to be free at the gas station. Now it's $1.80. You know why? Inflation.

There's that vegan girl again. I swear I've seen herbivore.

I didn't eat anything other than brown bread for lunch. That was my wholemeal.

I know nine months isn't that long, but it just feels like a maternity.

Most people are shocked when they find out how bad an electrician I am.

My friends all claim I'm the cheapest person they've ever met. I don't buy it!

I can't believe I got fired from the calendar factory. All I did was take a day off.

The police just pulled me over, and the officer came up to my window and said, "Papers?" I said, "Scissors, I win!" and drove off. He's been chasing me for 45 minutes now; I think he wants a rematch.

When two vegans get in an argument, is it still called a beef?

I was born to be a pessimist. My blood type is B Negative.

Two wind turbines stand in a field. One says to the other, "So, what kind of music are you into?" The other replies, "I'm a huge metal fan."

I thought about going on an all-almond diet. But that's just nuts.

My wife says I have an unhealthy obsession with revenge.
We'll see about that...

A dead battery walks into a bar and orders a beer. The barman says he won't take its money. "No charge."

Police Officer
I am arresting you for illegally downloading the entire Wikipedia.

Dad
Wait! I can explain everything!

A bossy man walks into a bar. He orders everyone a round.

I burned my Hawaiian pizza. I should have used aloha temperature.

So what if I don't know what apocalypse means? It's not the end of the world.

My boss asked me why I get sick only on workdays. I said it must be my weekend immune system.

A children's sports charity was fundraising. They were asking for donations for their new pool, so I gave them a cup of water.

Pride is what you feel when your kids net $150 from your yard sale. Panic is what you feel when you realize your barbeque is missing.

A pair of jumper cables walk into a bar. The barman tells them, "I'll serve you, but don't go starting anything."

After dinner, my wife asked if I could clear the table. I needed to take a big run at it, but I made it.

My doctor told me I'm starting to go deaf. The news was hard for me to hear.

Four golfers are standing under their umbrellas in the pouring rain, about to tee off. They look over to the river and say, "Have a look at those fools, fishing in this weather!"

I love telling Dad jokes.
Sometimes, he even laughs.

Not sure if you have noticed, but I love
bad puns. That's just how eye roll.

CONCLUSION

And here we are, over 300 dad jokes later, and we can still think of hundreds that didn't make the cut. This is the beauty of the perfect dad joke: fulfilling, yet quite infinite.

We won't keep you too long in this conclusion. What we have to say, however, is that you should never forget to use your dad joke power for good. Keep the jokes funny, keep the jokes light, and keep the jokes fresh. Leave the heavy stuff for the comedians (wait, we mean politicians).

We hope you had as much fun reading this book as we had writing it. Remember: The next time you are at an awkward thread party and need something to cut the tension, look for a pair of scissors (AKA, this book).

REFERENCES

100 of the Best Funny Puns (n.d.) Ponly.com https://ponly.com/funny-puns

40 Father's Day Jokes That Are Guaranteed To Get A Laugh by Kidadl. Kidadl.com. (2020, December 19) https://kidadl.com/articles/fathers-day-jokes-that-are-guaranteed-to-get-a-laugh

Funny Jokes About Jobs (n.d.). Keeplaughingforever.com. https://www.keeplaughingforever.com/corny-dad-jokes

Funny Puns (n.d.) Punpedia. https://punpedia.org/funny-puns

McKay, B. (2021, June 5). 20 Not (That) Lame Knock-Knock Jokes. The Art of Manliness.com. https://www.artofmanliness.com/living/games-tricks/best-knock-knock-jokes

The Best Corny Dad Jokes Of 2021 (n.d.). Keeplaughingforever.com. https://www.keeplaughingforever.com/job-jokes

Printed in Great Britain
by Amazon

14571427R00068